COUNTRY OF GOD

by Nawaf Haskan

2021 by Nawaf Haskan

Published by Giant Publishing Company
Post Office Box 6455
Lincoln, NE 68506
www.giantpublishingcompany.com

Printed in the United States of America

Cover photo by Christine van den Toorn. The author's family home, after ISIS blew it up.

Author's photo by Erin Trieb.

ISBN 978-1-7352827-4-9

Acknowledgments

I thank my American family (Bonny and Michael) for their kindness and generosity. They supported me and my wife (Laila) and let us stay in their home for nine months. By spending time with my American family, we have learned a lot about American life, culture, food, and politics.

My gratitude goes to **Jean Nordhaus** for giving me valuable advice about poetry and introducing me to American poets and poetry.

I also want to deeply thank my family in Iraq and the rest of the world. Despite all the difficulties they are facing, they are always there to help me and inspire me not to give up. Special thanks to my best friend, Peter Slemani.

Lastly, I would love to thank my wife, Laila, who has been the source of all my inspiration. Without her love, loyalty, and kindness, there would be no poem. I shall say to her, "You are a beautiful poem."

I dedicate this book to my daughters, Aya and Talia.

It is my wish that this book will reach the hands of many people and the memories of my Yazidi community and American community.

Poems

Five Sisters...7

A Date with Aleppo..9

Sinjar-LA's Monologue.....................................10

Standing People...12

Talking to Myself...14

Again & Again..15

Anecdotes...16

They..17

Conditions and Questions..................................18

A Fake Smile...19

HAY-LEY...20

Country of God...21

Situation...22

A Conversation With Mom..................................23

Those Who Are in Need.....................................25

In the Memory of an Interpreter, My Cousin...........26

Front Lines vs. My Grandfather...........................27

(4:30 am)..28

Starbucks Barista..29

Some Details...30

Destinies...31

Man's Tragedy...32

Happy Hour..33

Never New York..34

A Moment of Electronic Life..............................35

Happy V...36

What is a Poem?...37

A Talk With the Mountain.................................38

A Keyboarded Being..39

Lana...40

Customers...42

Poems, continued

Trapped..43
???...44
Trea..45
The New Sinjar...46
Nebraska..47
D.C..48

Five Sisters

Over there, in that sleeping town, beyond those
hills that lay down,
five sisters hurried to the naked mountain. Over
there, in that deserted land,
where short and long valleys walk together hand in
hand, where the plain has no grove and no green,
where dirt routes don't conclude, five sisters were
taken.
No one saved them.
The high and low mounds, the scattered oaks,
the rough and smooth rocks,
the immense and little, the stones, all these did not
save them.
Over there, in that grey-blue distance, five sisters
screamed.
Over there, five sisters were left behind,
five sisters were grabbed from the arms of their
family to face the guns' muzzles in a sunburnt
town,
in a far horizon, in a rugged mountain range.
God witnessed this tragedy,
the stunning moon witnessed it, the lithe
xerophytes witnessed it,
the salty warm dark soil witnessed it, the hot
golden noon witnessed it,
the ash houses, the dead bodies, the dusty air, the
blood's smell, and the sunbeams witnessed it.
None dared prevent it.
I did not: coward, feeble, poor sister.

What a nothing I am!
I wish I would be instead of them,
I wish I would not be born within this system,
under this sky, in this brown state,
and in this bloody kingdom
I wish I would die.
So, these homing thoughts could fly.

A Date with Aleppo

She stroked her clothes, looking for the right dress
She was not sure what to choose: The blue or the
pink?
The red or the yellow?
Should she pick a glossy dress or a frilly one?
After she chose his favorite color,
she put her valuables and not-so valuables in a
handbag. She grabbed a peep-toe pump shoe.
She should not forget the white pearl bracelet
and the red ruby heart promise ring that he gave
her last Valentine's Day.
She consulted the mirror for the last check. She
rushed outside to meet the beloved one. The only
one who has delighted her heart. Then, she
remembers her beloved is gone. There is no date
at all.
The only dress that she may put on is a shroud.
The only beloved one now is death.

Sinjar-LA's Monologue

Do you know who I am?
I am the heart that was burned looking for peace.
Not any peace, but your peace,
taking from your eyes its own beat.
I am the light that drove the darkness so insane
once, guiding the children their beds instead of the
graves.
I am the last mass-grave to be discovered, bringing
more sorrows.
I am the wound that bled 74 times in the absence
of your embrace.
I am the only fig tree that kept its fruit for the
brides to give to their bridegrooms on an Eid day.
I am the only smile that was taken away and never
put back until you remembered our date once
again.
Do you have an idea, now, who I am?
I am the only mountain that stood against an evil
god protecting infants, that they not be taken from
their moms.
I am the last puff of a Karse tobacco's cigarette to
inhale enjoying the last minutes of life with no
misery.
I am the boat that was lost for decades,
Sailing to meet the shore of you.

I am the existence that had no existence without your existence.
I am the poet who only wrote a few lines
And, then stopped and started waiting for your words. I am Sinjar, you LA.

Standing People

(1)
I was born standing.
I was weaned, standing.
I was educated, and I grew up standing.
(2)
I cried, grieved, laughed, and got bored, standing.
In my country, whatever a person does, he will do, standing.
(3)
I've loved and been loved. Even sex, I have practiced, standing.
They taught me speech, poetry, and writing.
Even praying and drunkenness, I have learned them standing. They put me into the school, the hospital, the p ark, a bar, then the nightclub, standing.
They taught me how to sleep, how to eat, and how to dance and sing, standing.
(4)
They walked me into the temple, the church, the mosque, standing.
They blessed me, called me the faithful. Then, they taught me deception, sedition, robbery, and even rape, standing.
They turned me into a soldier, a warrior, a patriot, and a terrorist, standing.
They taught me the art of slaughtering and killing, standing.

(5)

In my country, everything you learn and you do, you're going to do it, standing.

(6)

They've changed my identity, religion, and nationality. I was born as a Sumerian, Babylonian, and Assyrian, as a Yezidi, as a Christian and a Muslim, Sunni or Shia, then as an atheist and as a sectarian, standing.

They made me Arab, then Iraqi and then Kurdish, and finally, a stranger in my own country, standing.

(7)

In my country, whatever happens to a person, it happens to him, standing.

(8)

They elected me emperor, king, president, dictator, democrat, thief, and then slave, standing.

(9)

In my country, a person could be born, fall in love, live, be hung, be slaughtered, die, and even be buried, standing.

Talking to Myself

I am afraid of the silence that covers our faces
It precludes cries and smiles
It precludes sorrows and happiness, letting nothing
stay in our hands and within our trembling feelings
It makes us vainly collect the remains of words
and have a vile conversation with the rest of the
world
Hence, say something because silence scares me
It is the dagger that cuts our connections
It is the bell that warns of the collapse of our
togetherness
Say something, anything; all my feelings are
listening to yours

Again & Again

Again, the night has come back to kill the tumult
of the day,
To throw its serenity over the world far away
It also brought the sparrows back to the backyard
To plant some tunes on the branches of my only
tree
And I went to the window
To watch the darkness that surrounded me
And, to send the warn steam of my coffee with its
silence
Very carefully, the night sneaked in among my
things
It covered my face with the secrets of nature
It cleared my heart from the burden of everything I
lost
Beyond that gloomy darkness, I could not see
anything
The daisies darkened, and the rest of the flowers
slept
The fatigued tree wobbled
In this ongoing chaos, your face has appeared like
a sun that would rise in a minute and never set.

Anecdotes

(1)
With a shaking hand, she handed her not-smart phone to the young man behind the counter asked him to fix it. He checked the cellphone for several minutes and said, "Ma'am, there is nothing wrong with your phone!" She asked, "Then why do I not receive any phone calls from my children?!"

(2)
Sookie asked me,
 "Do you know who has the best life these days?" I answered, "No." She said, "The president's dog, who enjoys the White House with no clue how she got there."
I just realized that even dogs have a sense of humor.

(3)
My 4-year old nephew asked, "Do you know what happened to all the kings of ancient times?" I replied, "No idea." He
laughed, "Hahaha…they died." He asked again, "Do you know what happened to the people of ancient days, then?" I asked back, "What do you think?" He laughed again and said, "They also died...hahaha."

(4)
My friend who lost his whole family in the last genocide asked, "Why doesn't God reply to my prayers these days?" I replied, "We can visit His grave and ask Him."

They

Only they can disclose the secrets of our hearts
and articulate the moments we have counted in
each other's absence.
They only can know whom we longed for in a time
of no sense
and for whom we washed those walls with tears.
They set us in ages of patience waiting for seconds
to pass. They unveil our riddles and hide our facts.
If you ever doubted my love, question them?
They can tell you whom I thought of while waiting
for your steps to touch the land of my impatience.
They can enlighten you about the sadness that was
in my eyes while seeing left behind
or watching myself saying goodbye to the last
words you colored my heart with once
If you ever doubted,
Ask them why I was there five hours ahead? And
five hours behind?
Airports are bad witnesses to good love crimes.

Conditions and Questions

If you cannot be organized,
in a scattered world, what would you be? If you
cannot be stunning,
in an organized world, what would you be? If you
cannot be evasive in a gambling world, what
would you be? If you cannot be peaceful
in a world at war, what would you be? If you
cannot be a warrior in a teasing environment, what
would you be? If you cannot be a poet in the Fall,
what would you be? If you cannot be the Fall in a
year, what would you be?

If you cannot be,
What would you be?

A Fake Smile

Many things can be faked today,
But not a smile.
You can get fake news,
Have fake coffee to start your day,
Get a fake lottery email,
A fake credit or debit card,
A fake address,
A fake religion,
A fake identity card,
A fake relationship,
A fake Twitter or Facebook account,
You can even have a fake president.
But, what you cannot fake is to make: a smile!
The only reason that my grandmother could bear
my grandfather's snoring every night through 8
children and 47 grandchildren is that he had a real
smile.
That's how I know a smile cannot be faked. I have
my grandfather's curse.
Too serious about having a fake smile.
And, that's why at the last job, when they laid me
off telling me "You do not smile,"
I really laughed.

HAY-LEY

What should I call you?
A hand full of light that dispels the darkness, a
spirit of hope that nourishes my being,
or a breath that gives me life.
The flames of your love kill my grim expressions.
The brightness of your face shines in my realms.
The beauty of your eyes takes over the colors of
my Fall. And, the sweetness of your touch dries
up all my worries. An instant of reflection about
you, takes me back to the embrace of my
grandfather's olive tree. It sets off volcanoes of
love inside me.
It makes me high. What should I call you?
A word that is buried between my lips; the word
that only a kiss would revive, or a feeling that has
no rivals.
Since the begging and till this day,
You have remained as a secret in my mind, and an
eagerness that elates my heart.

Country of God

----- Over there, my friend, far away, is a country like a paradise, a country where eternal love exists.
----- Over there, my friend, is the homeland of roses and flowers, the homeland of freedom, good life, of wellbeing, and exceptional love. Would you, my friend, think with me for a moment about that immortalized paradise? Would you write some poetry or a poetic line about it? About the country of dreams, about the shores, the sea, about the high mountains and about the happy people.
----- Over there, my friend, far away in every inch, roses grow instead of briars, forests of incense instead of graves. Over there in God's holy land, life exists, welfare, fairies, scientists, queens, and even writers exist.
----- Over there, my friend, in the dove's nest, on the olive's stem, there is affluence, there are children, good people, and faithful people...
People who don't think about death, which are not terrified by madness... Wouldn't you like to be there?
----- In the view of many in this country, we are infidels, ignorant, dispossessed. In this country, we try to plant palms, but others spread fear and plant bombs, while we try to spread the love with kisses.

Situation One

She knows this will be the last time to see him.
She also knows if he leaves her this time, he will
never come back. She tries to talk to him, but the
tongue cannot form the words she wants. She tries
to hold his hand, but the place is semi-public, and
dozens of eyes watch. She wants to say goodbye
with a hug, a kiss, or the last touch; but, she
hesitates: in her society, hugs, kisses, and touches
occur only in private.
For the last time, she wants to lie down beside him
and put her head on his chest to feel the remaining
heat in his body. But again, she remembers that, in
her community, such acts are prohibited except in
darkness. She tries to kiss his forehead.
She hesitates again: a woman can only be kissed;
she cannot kiss.
Nurses come to take his body out of her hands
before she can do what was in her mind.
Her thoughts turn into tears that fall on my white
paper: record the history of a lover who leaves her
beloved to face life's last tragedy alone.

A Conversation with Mom

(1)

She tells me not to worry
"Everything is going to be all right." But how?
When tears rest on my cheeks,
and my heart is full of pain and sorrow. How?
When fear fills my chest these days,
and ghosts visit me, while I am overtaken by
phantoms.

(2)

She again, "Don't worry. We will be fine!" How?
When nothing good comes out of my homeland,
and in the spring of my youth, I feel each day is
my end. Just how?
When death walks by my front door, when I've
become its prisoner.

(3)

Yet again, she says, "Don't worry; happiness is
knocking at the door."
How?
While everything in my country has become terror.
Religion, politics, faith, nationality,
and even love, in my country, all turned to
terrorism. How?
When the faithful one has become an executioner,
and buildings have become shambles.

(4)

She looks at me with tearful eyes… talking to
herself tearful eyes, she mutters:
"No, No, we are not all right," "We are not fine,"

"And happiness doesn't knock at the door." I ask her, "Are you okay?"

She smiles, and says, "Yes, son, I said, don't worry, we'll be all right!"

Those Who Are in Need

There are those people who are in need of many
things.
Such as a small radio and two extra batteries,
A notebook to write down some poetry or a diary,
a pen and no eraser,
Or a small lamp, some gasoline, and a very dark
room.
…..
There are those who are in need of some beautiful
things; such as a small smile and healthy teeth.
…..
There are those who are in need of valuable things;
such as a small house and a secured country.
…..
There are those who are in need of other things;
such as a revolver and one single bullet.

In the Memory of an Interpreter, My Cousin

Here he walks, leaving behind him a beautiful laugh, sweet memories, a very touching memoir. Each moment that he lived was a lifetime. He was like a prophet whom God sent to be loved.

No one knows what he may be in a place other than his, in a country that does not resemble his homeland and in a time that is not like the moments of his life. Everyone cried, but only fate laughed.

Front Lines vs. My Grandfather

My grandfather forced me to walk five miles every day to the school for 12 years to keep me away from the front lines.

He died, and the front lines came to me.

(4:30 am)

The time I wake up more than any other hour in
my life.
Once to drink milk,
Once to sell milk,
Once to drink coffee,
Today, to sell coffee.

Starbucks Barista

I made a lot of coffee today.
So tired that I hated the world.
So tired that I needed a huge hug from my mother.
So tired, I wanted to sleep and never wake up.
When I came home, my wife asked me, "Why
don't we have a kid?"
There are questions that need answers.
But, there are more answers that need to be
questioned?

Some Details

We fall in love with those who care about the
minute details of our life:
Our favorite book, that song we love, our favorite
drink, birthday present, the color of our socks, our
hairstyle, the brand of perfume or toothpaste we
use, and even our moments of silence.

The love that lacks these trivial details lacks a lot.

Destinies

John has never liked to ride on buses.
Yet he became the driver of the biggest bus in the
city.
It was John's destiny to become a bus driver.
Saeed hated math. Yet he is the only math teacher
in the town.
It was Saeed's destiny to be a math teacher.
Laila spoke no English.
It was Laila's destiny to become an English
reporter.
And, it is my destiny to give away love for a very
high price.

Man's Tragedy

My father defended his country for thirteen years,
then they abandoned him, destroyed his farm, and
tried to kill his whole family.
But, he still has a keen sense of belonging to his
homeland.
The tragedy of a man in his homeland.

Happy Hour

A healthy dinner, some spinach salad, and a cup of
ouzo.
An interesting conversation about the last novel I
read,
The flavor of seafood and the sound of the sea's
pacific wave,
Sephardic music and the voice of Yasmin Levy
while she sings in Ladino: "I drink and drink to
forget you"... "Damn you."

The most beautiful evening for the remnants of
some people from the remnants of a devastated
homeland ...

Never New York

You stare at nothing,
listening to the silence of the words.
You have ended up in the middle of a strange city,
knowing nothing about her braids.
You give people you do not know their language
and their silence your smile,
waiting to encounter a familiar face. A breeze
crashes into your face,
and a dream comes to you, so you remember her.
You remember that you had a woman, you loved
her in a crazy way.
These memories run with each breeze, as swarms
of birds.
taking you back to a past when you were dancing
with her on the palm of a Goddess
and when you would sleep between her shoulders
on the shoulder of a mountain.
So, you smile at the tumble that happened to her in
Bari. You remember her laugh as she picks up figs
with her fingertips – angelic ones.
You remember her saying, "I love this place more
than New York."
The sound of the metro wakes you up from such a
dream.
Then you know you are in New York, and she lies
peacefully in the center of that dead mountain.

A Moment of Electronic Life

I hate this electronic life. I was not born American to deal with all these apps. I am the one who was used to family gatherings. Today, if I want to tell my mom about my downfalls, I must send her a sad face or a face with tears, a stupid emoji.

Before I would go to her, jump into her arms and cry between her arms. She would wipe off my tears, give me a hug and a kiss, and I would be fine for the rest of the week or month.

Happy V

I jilt grief,
revolting against mourning.
I chased the nymph of the day, crossing the juggle
of time.
I yearn for your deep voice, shaking in the cold
tears of the sun.
I dive into the corners of the poems remembering
all our sweet moments, our home, farm, and
flowers,
and my grandfather's angelic face, the rain that
showered the sidewalks
and the snow that covered the mountain's
shoulders.
Now, you come in on an undecided date on an
unusual day to tell me something that
"Conversation's Hearts" of the Valentine's Day do
not have yet
and something beyond what they sing in the
Valentine' s mornings.
You ring the bell of an open door
and with a gorgeous smile, you pour the sky into
my hands or something so like a dream that even
the heart's shores forgot it.
Oh you, the one who takes me on a skiff to
nowhere and everywhere.

What is a poem?

A poem should warm the hearts of lovers.
She should burst one's thoughts.
She should hold people's lives.
A poem should act like a Goddess.

She should burst one's thoughts.
A poem should never pass away.
A poem should act like a Goddess
She should be remembered every day.

A poem should never pass away.
She should be the source of happiness.
She should be remembered every day.
A poem should remind you of Venus.

She should be the source of happiness.
A poem should remind you of Nora.
A poem should remind you of Venus.
She should remind you of Flora.

A poem should remind you of Nora.
She should embody a Goddess.
She should remind you of Flora.
A poem should give birth to other Goddesses.

A Talk with the Mountain

Talk to me, Jabal Sinjar, the father of all
mountains.
You are the only one who was washed by their
blood,
and the only one who swallowed their skinny
bodies.
You embraced them and by their palms your face
was touched.

So, you may keep them.
But, you did not protect them as you promised.
How dare you not to protect them?
Is it because you yourself were dead too?

Talk to me, say some names.
Talk to me, whenever you dare to talk.
Show me some bones.
Say something, or maybe say nothing and do not
even speak.

A Keyboarded Being

If we only put our keyboards aside
and our momentarily feelings aside,
If we put our technical unawareness aside, if only,
this life will be so lovely.

If we only can take the justice side,
If we only can exchange forgiveness with apology,
If we could or can look back once and forward
twice,
If we could tie ourselves to our human nature
merely,

The world would be ours.

Lana

Lana follows my steps and spies on my
movements.
Lana steals my breath... and robs me of my senses.
Lana makes me tired... Lana makes me weary.
Lana confiscates all my dictionaries, takes over my
words and writes off all the sentences.
Lana kills me and my silence.
Lana hangs me... Lana warps my thoughts and
erases my journals.
Lana deprives me of my sleep, my doze and
awakens.
Lana makes love with me every night... and rapes
me every night.
Lana deprives me from my prayers... and forbids
my prayers.

Lana, Lana, who is Lana?

Lana sits with me in my meetings... next to me and
behind me.
Lana passes behind me and in front of me.
Lana talks to me, makes me laugh and cry.
Lana fascinates me with her smile,
with her perfume, and with her looks.
Lana drives me crazy with her dramatic gestures
and her winks.
I do not even know who Lana is!
Lana and whoever Lana is.
Lana makes me travel to the farthest place, the

worst place, and the most beautiful place.

Lana makes me give up my religion, my ethnicity, and insults my nationality.

Lana pushes me to commit the biggest crime, and the worst crime.

Lana demonizes me.

In Lana's eyes, there are thousands of stories, anecdotes, and poems.

But I do not know what is hidden in Lana's heart, because I do not know who the hell Lana is!

Customers

The cute kid
The beautiful young blonde lady
The smart senior boy
The old funny guy
and, the old rich bitch who gives no tips!

Trapped

Maybe it is the time to give the midnight moon
with a goodbye kiss,
and a hug to the afternoon sun.
Maybe it's the time to surrender to the earth for
good.
But, the sun here is cold for a hug and the moon is
so dark.
And, the earth here does not welcome strangers.

The Mother Earth is frustrated by what the Father
Sky does, and I am trapped in between.

???

In a world with no man but me
With a heart full of mercy
On a moment of peace,
I saw you tiptoeing through my life.

On your arrival,
The storm hit, the heart palpitated,
a war started, and more men were born.
Yet, I was delighted.

Then, slowly, your image faded away.
The quietness swallowed the remains of the
thunder.
Men were buried into peace.
And my heart started the eulogies.

Unfortunately, I am at age of life where I have to
sing a song,
Where I have to say something,
Where I have to either let you go for
the sake of peace!
Or keep you for my sake!

Why not stay?
Why not go away?
Why did you come on the first day?

Trea

Longed for that heart's beats.
Longed for the beauty of those eyes.
Longed for saying "Hi the dearest" many more
times.

Longed for those old days.
Longed for Fairuz's songs in your voice.
Longed for the hope that shined in your smiles.
Longed to your every tiny thing.
Longed to those unfinished walks.

Longed for a sit on the blue chairs,
The cafeteria smells,
The sad yellow walls.
Longed to yours.

Isn't it time to go back?
To sum up that talk?
To finish the unfinished walk?

The New Sinjar

In my last visit to Sinjar, I hated it a lot.
Sinjar without you does not mean anything to me.
The cities where no poet is and are not in love with
are dead cities,
The cities where poets do not visit and meet are
dead cities.
I visited the same school where we studied and sat
in that same seat.
I remembered our talk about books that were
burned in libraries of our country.
About the friends who were martyred in its
trenches,
And about the students who were killed in its
schools,
About the faces of the widows,
About political drama,
About the kind of smoke we secretly inhaled
behind the school fence!
And about the girls we loved
I remembered all these and then drowned in my
loneliness.

Nebraska

Everyone will be going away
Carrying their own sorrows
But, we will keep the music and dance for another
century.
———-

Another very cold winter will come
And l will feel the cold climbing my bones
Covers after covers but I won't feel my body
It is damn Nebraska.

D.C.

DC, my favorite unfavorite destination.
The city that sleeps on promises and wakes up on
lies,
The snake's head hole
The top and the bottom
DC, the old annoying mother-in-law
The mother and the daughter
The birth of a bad plan for a long war in a peaceful
planet
The scar of power and shame
The wife and the second wife
The venue of a change and challenge
The Potomac, the White House and the no house
The fancy and the ugly.